What's Left

poems by

Tate Lewis-Carroll

Finishing Line Press
Georgetown, Kentucky

What's Left

Copyright © 2023 by Tate Lewis-Carroll
ISBN 979-8-88838-078-9 First Edition
All rights reserved under International and Pan-American Copyright Conventions. No part of this book may be reproduced in any manner whatsoever without written permission from the publisher, except in the case of brief quotations embodied in critical articles and reviews.

Publisher: Leah Huete de Maines
Editor: Christen Kincaid
Cover Art: Izzy Lewis-Carroll
Author Photo: Izzy Lewis-Carroll
Cover Design: Elizabeth Maines McCleavy

Order online: www.finishinglinepress.com
also available on amazon.com

Author inquiries and mail orders:
Finishing Line Press
P. O. Box 1626
Georgetown, Kentucky 40324
U. S. A.

Table of Contents

Shell Collecting 1

Chemo 3

My Father was a Skipped Rock 11

At My Father's Wake 13

Vader 14

Ventilator 15

I Dreamt us Having a Pure Son and Father Moment 17

MRI 20

The Anatomical Man, ... 21

Peonies in Reverse 23

To My Father's Roses 24

At My Father's Wake 25

Pure Land 26

Olive Oil with Balsamic 28

At My Father's Wake 29

Silent Flight: Sestina 30

The Final Day 32

My Father's Needlepointed Santa Lumbar Pillow 33

Black Bird 34

The Number One Rule in Poetry 35

Practice: Haiku 38

At My Father's Wake… 41

Crows 42

His Iowa Friends 43

At My Father's Wake… 44

River 46

Sometime After My Father Died 47

What's Left 48

Another Cherry Tree 49

Clear 57

In The Lens 59

At My Father's Wake… 60

Memorial Day 61

Nullipara 62

Aubade 63

Alphabet Cone 64

Acknowledgments 67

I tried hard   to have   a father
but instead I   had   a dad

—Nirvana

Hey Tatey
    uh

        it's your dad

thanks for calling
  um

    call me back and
    uh
    we can talk a little bit

alright buddy

    thanks
    bye

—Jim Lewis

Shell Collecting

In Florida, my father's hands hardly rested.
Before sunrise, they would be the first to open,
knuckle the boozy sleep from his eyes,
scratch his rear, creak open my door,
pull my covers away, and carry me
from bed alongside our flashlights
and plastic grocery bags all the way
down the boardwalk to the Gulf
where we would stalk the beach, hunting
for shells.

In the still forming twilight,
his hands would hover above the water,
swinging the flashlight, searching—
Suddenly they would dig,
sift, pluck, and cradle shells that hid from us
like the right word for a poem: *precious wentletrap,
lettered olive, moon snail.* He'd recall their names
as if he were the one who'd lost them.

Once, I found an elusive, living lace murex,
dyed with auburn streaks. Its pink foot
pig-tailed out of its shell onto my palm.
A family trick passed down from my mother's side
for situations like this would be to boil it
and then fish out the cooked creature with a fork.
Of course, I asked him if we could
because I thought I couldn't let it go.

For a moment, his hands rested
on my shoulders. Then he said, *No.
How would you like to be boiled and displayed?*
He chuckled, *You better not ever do that to me,*
and motioned for me to put it back.
I nodded, bent down, and slipped it into my pocket.

It is now week whatever in the ICU,
and this is the closest he's been to death,
desperate for a new liver. Feeding tubes
reach from his nostrils to his stomach.
The ventilator has been operating for days.
Someone just catheterized both his bladder and heart.
The port below his collarbone is two fingers wide.
Needles pierce his neck, forearm, thumb, and groin.

His shriveled hands catch the slow drip of chemo
and fill with bruises like the rest of his body.
Med teachers have designated him a manikin
for their students to practice drawing blood
or injecting medicines without collapsing his veins
before they move on to more aware patients.

Sometimes, groups of first years, drawn by rumors
or led by a fellow student, will crowd the doorway
and gaze at his jaundiced glow filtered through a bruised
smog, haloing him, and quietly gasp, *Beautiful*—

Chemo

Cancer is a motorcycle
speeding,
splitting
sticky, summer
sun, sideways
somersaulting.

Chemo is the rake
of concrete
scratching out
both the corroded
ride and crooked
rider—

It does not distinguish
upholstery from skin,
coils from marrow,
spokes from teeth.

Now, in the ICU,
the treatment
for the disease
he raised
instead of me
halves him

quarters him

eighths him

sixteenths him

thirty-seconds him

sixty-fourths him

one-hundred-twenty-eighths him

two-hundred-fifty-sixths him

My Father was a Skipped Rock

Proudly, slapping the water,
he taught me how to sail.
With his hands cupping mine,
we gripped the tiller,
dodged the boom,
maneuvered over white-capped swells
surging through northern and biting winds,
on days it seemed we could see
further down into Lake Michigan
than up into the sky.

Sometimes, far beyond the breakwall,
the lighthouse bobbing in and out of sight,
he would let the sail slack.
With a bottle to his lips
he assured me it was alright,
> *only a taste,*
> > *a nip,*
> *a mouthful,*
> > *a swallow,*
> *a slug,*

then another.

Truthfully, it never concerned me,
but one day he hid my life jacket
and forbade me from following.
I don't know what pushed him to launch alone
from then on, skimming toward deeper,
more unforgiving waters.

Then summer,
bedridden and sickly,
decayed into autumn,
coughed out phlegm and bile
until winter hardened the wind,
sails, swells, boom, tiller,
and him into stone.

My father was a skipped rock—
sinking.

At My Father's Wake (An Exhibit Where Strangers Stick Their Fingers in My Cage to Feed Me Their Opinions Disguised as Pieties)

God, you need a haircut.
It's really looking bad
at that length. No offence.
Sorry for your loss.

Vader

The Force
failed us.
I searched
my feelings,
but nothing
could prepare
my own eyes
for his
tear-crusted
crows-feet,
the dried vomit
in his stubble,
his pale body
crumpled
on the floor,
fighting
just to breathe.
How could that man—
who dispensed
with the pleasantries,
who plagued
even the Outer Rim
with his anger,
who lured me
into trap after trap,
who never
set his weapons
to stun,
who I swore
to defeat—
ever restore balance?
And why is
the cure darker
than the disease?

Ventilator

in
his gelatinous ton—
out
—gue swells and
in
he drowns un—
out
—til the ventil—
in
—ator activates
out
his breath
in
refuses to sh—
out
—iver or shift
in
or coil
out
like dande—
in
—lion paratrooper's
out
chaos in
in
invading late May
out
instead, his scar—
in
—red lungs fill
out
with sterile
in
barren air
out
his tube
in

hums and dr—
out
—ags him a—
in
—long like a pit
out
bull on a ch—
in
—ain and d—
out
—angles death
in
be—
out
—yond his leash

I Dreamt Us Having a Pure Son and Father Moment

A reversed perspective of Kent Johnson's "I Dreamt Us Having A Pure Father And Son Moment"

I dreamt us having a pure son and father moment
too, but near the boundary waters where cross-stitched roots
pull islands into paths. I prepared to listen
by filling swarms of mosquitoes
with mantras, hymns, chants, prayers, and blood
sacraments. I counted their bloated bodies
drifting away to spread the news: 7,346,235,014.

When ready, you asked, *What was it like?*
and I opened my ribcage, and you pulled
out enchanted beasts: loons sliding into the muck
to milk their eggs; walleyes floating up the jack pines
to fill their nests with leftover fly paper and splintered
ax handles and used handkerchiefs discarded by Eagle
Scouts; ducks with lion teeth; beavers dreaming
of planting trees in their sleep; coyotes and foxes boxing
with their hind legs, bumble bees with cormorant wings
tap dancing on top of cattails—You took them
one by one until the magic was gone.

With my cage open I said, *Look into my eyes.*
You looked down, away from me, though I knew
you knew how lucidly I saw your face reflected
in the glass lake next to my own. And at that moment,
at once, together, our tears met their rising echoes
in ripples on our cheeks. They rose and rose and fell
and rose.

You tried to convince me your tears were for me,
always slipping throughout you instead of your rage
then sadness then shame (I assume shame)—
the snarling emptied between us. But tears never curve.
      We only ever cry into our own reflections.

Clouds below us, the shared space, swelled with our penitence.
Then you soaked your palms in my reflection
to cover the distance and dry my face,
but you felt foreign, and I felt nothing,
and this dream, our reaching and drowning
into each other, ever rushing towards its end,
has never stopped or changed, either,
no matter how much I have wanted to wake.

MRI

The technician plunges contrast into his IV and slides him into that blaring, magnetic whirlwind. Mottled lakes of bleached yellow connected by streams of running purples and washed blues digitalize in front of the technician's eyes. He records each brush stroke of the cancer's masterpiece, painting over his once grey, blank-canvas body. It's obvious the disease scattered through him like a buckshot to the gut since his last doctor's visit. He still hungers for food but it doesn't stay down. Even sips of milk, sometimes cut with water, reappear ropy and chalky on the point of his unshaven chin. His once olive skin, taut across his arms, now quivers with his failing strength and hangs pale, clothes spinned from his bones. The malignant pale gathers in his liver, the lump's pallet, then percolates into each lobe, each lymph node, each branch organ, each muscle. He focuses on the magnet above; rotating faster, wilder, replacing the sun's crepuscular climbing and diving horizon. Every turn plunders hours away from his life in seconds. Nothing can stop his final months from dusting out to free each .Th technician reminds him to hold still, the p or trait isn't finished yet. Supine, all my father can do is wait for his world to stop spinning.

20

The Anatomical Man,

reprinted as a blank outline
of himself in this oncology ward,
with open arms, clipped to a rugged

clipboard, welcomes my father
the same as all the other patients
who keep arriving one after another

to pen their pains onto his paper skin.
Without any protest, he accepts
each of them with promises of relief.

But the hard-wooded cross
he schleps into every exam room
never lightens any loads.

Peace of mind is only peace of mind,
designedly subminimal,
manufactured in mass

like medicine, but less effective.
Prayer didn't alter any medical test
nor scrape together one measly

hour more. Cancer does not obey any god
but itself. And what a jealous god
it is, always taking, taking.

With a jealous god come commands,
come severed limbs, come rivers
of blood, comes seeing the devil's hand

and raising it by boils, blistering
with heavenly confidence
across any faithful servant's back.

But say, in the end, God does take the pot,
the dice are loaded in his favor.
What cut of the prize is this suffering worth?

Peonies in Reverse

June, going on May, bowed bushes, heavy with pink
tissue crowns, follow the sun east

from my back yard and repel fluttering monarchs
whose antennae propel them backwards into the sky

toward their mending chrysalises where they fold
their delicate wings and re-liquefy.

The mosquito, smeared across my arm, shimmies
her thorax, legs, wings, compound eyes, feelers

back into their proper positions, while her proboscis
re-pierces my arm and returns her bloody-mary

into my diminishing welt before whining away
to scratch out the next name from her long list of amends.

The ruffled layers of carpels and cupped petals curl,
constricting into buds; fists of impacted matter.

A legion of ants, marching backwards from the ends
of crimping leaves, ransack their tunneled strongholds,

already flooding with the sour incontinence of root systems.
The bush's withering stems continue to shrink

until even a kaleidoscoping cloud of gnats could snap them.
Peonies in reverse—not unlike my father's sigh

when a surgical resident explained why
a younger patient took his place on the transplant list.

To My Father's Roses

Are the less-than-lovelies pruned,
one by one, anymore?
Have you tasted new dirt yet?
If not, then what's stopping you
from crowding the overgrown yard
with pink landing pads? Why stay
where his burrowing fingers shaped for you
both a muddy uterus and a seedy grave?
Break out of your brick bedroom,
silage sheets, mulch mattress,
and earthy pillows! Still, I understand
your relief in swilling gutter water,
dropping petals, oh, how he'd growl
at our unkemptness. Do stray cats,
the ones he used to chase away, now strip
your roots while digging for rabbit nests
and remind you of how he'd splinter
your twig arms, smile when you broke,
and crack open another drink?

At My Father's Wake (A Causeway Toll for which Passersby must Scrounge for Spare Remarks In Order to Leave the Island)

I'm just here for your brother,
I can't remember if I met your dad.
I might have met him at your bro's
wedding actually…anyways,
sorry for your loss.

Pure Land

Upon viewing Kano Hideyori's Maple Viewing at Mount Takao

Instead of The Golf Channel he slept through,
he stands at the foot hills of Mount Takao
with arms stretched upwards, watching white herons
and geese announce our arrival to the cherry blossoms,
lilies of the valleys, wild cherries, passion-flowers, and roses
who sing, with silky breaths, their perfume into the breeze
with sweet summer eagerness.

Instead of chilled beer poured in a frozen glass,
he drinks hot tea—its wisps of steam, warm and pleasant
and inviting, curl with the outline of his mustache—
and it opens him up the way a fighting conch stretches
out of its shell to dance in the current, loosening
his grip once clenched behind his barricade door, exposing
his soft pink and orange tenderness.

Instead of folding hands and kneeling behind a pew,
he dances in a circle, kicking around mud under visions of the Pure
Land breaking through the clouds beside the sun's ascension
in the east, drying the morning's dew, exposing permanent
meadows softened with running rivers, teaching dharmas,
inventing games for the gathered like a laughing Buddha,
like a father.

Olive Oil with Balsamic

Bottled within:
an inseparable
  duality,
       staining
and   spreading
  when tipped,
       then
obedient
  again
when righted—
the lightness rises
as, underneath,
the darkness settles.

At My Father's Wake (A Performance that Rarely Justifies the Line to the Box Office or the Price of Admission)

The playlist is perfect.
Your dad loved music.
We'd spend hours
just listening. Drugs
may or may not
have been involved.
You seem old enough
to know.
Condolences.

Silent Flight: Sestina

Among the whirring hospital equipment, his watch,
with hands tightened into fists, swinging and beating
against the glass, kept rhythm for his heart's pulsing music
I must have heard, though the notes were too weak for my ear.
But not to the asymmetrical ears of an owl,
rivaling any surgeon with their laparoscope, the fine work

of a scalpel to a patient laid bare. *This will work,*
I was repeatedly assured, *just wait, pray, and watch.*
But death had already whipped its head around like an owl,
pinpointing its prey among the prairie's smallest heartbeats.
With a guitar, I used to be able to learn songs by ear.
Sometimes, he would have me play along with his music

in the garage while he smoked cigars. *Your music,
Tatey, is worth all the practice and hard work
you got. Don't give up on it.* In the ICU, riffing next to his ear,
he no longer recognized the songs nor turned his face to watch
my fingers curl into chords or the scales beaten
on the neck. This is how he died, like an owl

silently taking flight. On the leading edges of a nocturnal owl's
wings are comb-like serrations, think eyelashes, which muffles its music
of flight so much so that each beat
is undetectable. I have long been fascinated by the workings
of silent flight from when he would take me bird-watching.
We would practice identifying calls with only our ears.

But now there's a constant ringing in my ears,
like the screeching call of a barn owl,
from a gun I once shot. Through the sights, I watched
a raccoon recoil; crumple. I cried. I've always used his music
to conjure him so as to comfort me, and it usually worked,
but it did nothing then to make that raccoon's heart re-beat.

It died, he died, and all the melodies, harmonies, beats
shattered, rained, articulate as ashes poured from an urn, onto my eardrums,
no longer able to perform their pitch-driven work.
An unsuspecting mouse never heard the owl
diving toward its heart, strumming that quiet music.
The fists slacked in his watch.

We can never fully know an owl's silent music,
but watching his body quit as machines beat his heart
re-trained my ears to listen for silence—my father's final work.

The Final Day

> *Death it seems was kinder to him in his last hour*
> *than life in his last four months*
> —Cornelius Eady

And at last, I received the phone call. The question
sank into my weary ear in an equally weary sob,
Do we let him die on his own now? We'd waited
the obligatory twenty-four hours for brain activity
        and nothing—not even a spark.
I had been afraid death would panic
when it finally realized its own end neared
alongside with my father's. I had assumed
it would riot furiously through his bloody streets,
loot his last operating organs for small change,
needlessly rip and clog until he's nobody.
        But I was wrong. Death, as I heard it, treated him right.
Finally wrapping those persistent arms around his chest,
it pulled him down into the sheets, laid out one last rebellion
to finally split from his toxic marriage to medicine—
from their household of one-sided diagnoses and empty treatments—
To go and go now, together, with what I'd once
believed was a poison, but now seems a healing.
I was told he went without hesitation,
even leaving the relief resting on his face
all the way to the crematorium.

My Father's Needlepointed Santa Lumbar Pillow

Deft fingers pushed the needle with its trail of thread in,
through, and back around, leaving little unpunctured:

the white puff on the stocking hat, the aging eyebrows,
the black dots of pupils, nostrils, and buttons running the length

of the velvet suit, and even though my father jabbed at
and smashed the pillow down towards his ass when he drove,

suppressing its incessant creep out of place up his spine
or down into the cloth seat, pinning it against the ache,

Santa kept grinning and lugging around that plush
sack, overflowing with teddy bears,

rocking horses decorated in baby blue bows,
skateboards, rattling beads, and loosening stitches

while raccoons and squirrels ducked to avoid his black boots
and the crow and owl on either shoulder craned their heads away.

At the exact moment of his death, when the weight of his body lifted,
he received the gift of finally and gently decompressing.

Black Bird

After The Beatles' Black Bird

Drench my skin in bee stings
and squid ink. Separate my flesh
and rip my veins. Clean me,
then keep going. Turn my body

into a canvas and tattoo this pain
on me so I cannot forget.
No color. No brashness. Just black.
Blacker than the quiet light

escaping from the heart of the wilderness
at the sun's routine turn.
Hauntingly black like a shadow
ducking behind corners, beyond

vision. Like a black bird, greased
and crooked, mother nature's
drunken muscle. Perch it
close to my ear. Make it weep

raspy songs in between drags
of cigarettes and pulls of dark
liquor until I fall asleep to the song
my father would sing to me:

> *Black bird singing*
> *in the dead of night—*
> *take these sunken eyes*
> *and learn to see—*
>
> *all your life.*

Remind and comfort me—
He always waited for this moment
to be free.

The Number One Rule in Poetry

For Mike Theune

When my fatherless father
        succumbed to his treatments

for the cancer,
        I wadded up

the snow-laced prairie
        like scrap paper.

But he picked it up,
        smoothed away the creases

on the edge of his desk.
        More, he said.

Show—don't tell—
        me more.

Then the snow sublimed.
        Chlorophyll fountained

in the paper's wrinkled heart.
        A blizzard of juncos

turned back north.
        It's easy to mistake them

for a creaking forest,
        chirping in the wind.

Somewhere cherry blossoms
        blossom again.

Somewhere moonshine
        is plenty.

What if we didn't crucify
 and worship what's fleeting?

Practice: Haiku

darkness—
I cannot imagine
nothing

———

sunrise—
the neighborhood
blushes

———

the hospital calls…
milk left on the counter
spoils

———

my first visit
to the hospital
wasn't his first trip

———

leaf hopper
after throwing itself
into the web

———

a ball of twine—
holding nothing together
but itself

———

windy morning—
harvested fields
fill with litter

———

like gardeners
but paid more—
surgeons

———

red sea
rushing back
to the heart

———

at lunch,
nursing students practice
on an orange

———

in the cafeteria—
familiar face,
avoiding eye-contact

———

they march single-file
into the chapel—
ants

———

computer died—
open outlet adjacent
the heart monitor

———

sudden rain—
the tree trunks darken
      the lichen lightens

———

after the storm—
a sunset
in every puddle

———

flowers bloom
in graveyards—
bees don't mind

———

October—
trees on fire remembering
my father's cremation

At My Father's Wake (An Arcade With Only *Whac-A-Mole* Machines)

> *I didn't even know Jim*
> *was sick and then all of a sudden*
> *I see his picture in the newspaper?*
> *Why didn't you tell me?*
> *If you'd've told me I could've*
> *done something helpful,*
> *but it doesn't matter now*
> *does it?*

Crows

They are not butterflies,
spirits of renewal, flapping
newly developed wings,
nor buzzards, spirits of rot,
drifting on tattered, black sails,
nor pin-pricked flecks
of death—they simply crave it.
They are the hissing gallery,
jeering, rooting, chanting
while they watch us die.

My father would point them out,
Look, they beat us here—
they are the first to circle down
from the trees in the morning,
fiercely beating their chests
and mocking the doves—
We all have something to mourn.

Each one is a perfect representation
of itself, hunching shoulders,
hopping limps, murders flocking
along highways to scatter
the remains of roadkill
before rising like smoke
from the wildfires in the gizzards,
seeking a barren tree
to clothesline their shadows.

They met me at my father's funeral.
I asked them, *How far have you traveled?*
What happens when a body rots?
Does a noticing soul ever blind?
They escorted me across the parking lot,
nodding, bowing, and gargling bones.

His Iowa Friends

After the funeral, after our friends
and families shuffled dully down the line
to take our hands, after brewing a fresh,
stale pot of coffee, after the playlist had repeated
again, they barged into the room, laughing
like tornado sirens shaking awake a sleepy town.

Although I had never met them before I recognized
their weight, rocking from bad knee to worse knee,
how they crossed and re-crossed their arms,
how they flashed toothy, salesmen grins, fired
finger guns, leaned away to check their watches
and the exit, one foot already out the door.

They came that afternoon to say goodbye,
but none made it past hello, tee time,
ex-wives, *Go Hawks*, or, *I don't know,
we never talked about that, we're not chicks*—
that familiar discomfort with conversation
heavier than ash.

At My Father's Wake (A Maze of *Fun House Mirrors* that Only Trusts its Own Reflections)

> *Knew him in college. Junior*
> *when I was a freshman.*
> *Some good times. You know,*
> *he was more of a guy's guy.*
> *Understand? Never got the whole*
> *family thing. Not because of you*
> *or anything. Feel better.*

River

        Dying is not
         like a river
          smoothing away
          a stone's history
         of roughness,
        nor is it the roar
       and plummet
      of a waterfall.
     No, at the end
    of the quick
   current, past
   the false turns
  and rapids,
there are shallows,
rippling alcoves
where all the
churned-up
 gravel collects.
That is where
  salmon finish their run
    and arrange their redds,
      near the same gravel beds
       where they hatched. My
        father was not one
       of those instinctive
        parents, guided upstream
       by some mysterious
      inner pull. No,
    he was at best
   a grizzly,
   jockeying
  for the prime
 fishing spot,
 unaware
of the poachers'
traps.

Sometime after My Father Died

I follow a creek through the woods.
Mud smacks, squelches, and suction-cups
to my boots. I come across a fallen
tree clinging to the river bank. Its gnarled,
serpent roots dip and curl through the murky grass.
Its spongey trunk sunk into the loose ground.
Lowering myself, I lay my hands on this giant
and admire bees alighting on almost unfurled-
ferns, birds hopping around its leaves,
mushroom umbrellas drying after the rain.
I make sure to withhold hope. It is not an answer
to anybody's prayers, and neither am I.
We are only other bodies paying respects
and resting on limbs.

    On its back,
    under thick
    patches of moss,
    on every trail, death
    again and again.

What's Left

My father left his eyes,
some framed
in wood and glass,
some spilled into boxes
with his clothes
        and flight manuals
                and metal figurines.

Meditations
            on
frosted pine trees—
what else besides perfect?
    Others
          refuse
enough.

        Cities aren't that big—
        hills still surround them.
    Snow falls
on mountains
      and my lips.

    If I had a peaceful heart it would look like this.

Sharks are born   swimming
birds are born   singing
we are born   dying

Another Cherry Tree

Upon viewing Luther Burbank *by Frida Kahlo*

"As a scientist, I cannot help feeling that all religions are a tottering foundation. I am an infidel today. I do not believe that what has been served to me to believe. I am a doubter, a questioner, a skeptic. When it can be proved to me that there is immorality, that there is resurrection beyond the gates of death, then will I believe. Until then, no."
—Luther Burbank

Enough.
The dead are dead and remain dead,
and after all these years of obsession—
the dreadful fear of losing a single shade
on the palette of his memories—
he's finally dull. A foggy coastline.
But there's rain on new flourishes of inspiration,
budding up around me, and so I am ready
to let him go.

Under a newly warm spring sun, I skip
to my blue shed to grab my shovel,
hanging on the wall in-between my metal rake and ax,
before heading out back by the garden
to dig.

I dig and dig and finally I'm sweating
in the damp, cool air at the bottom of a hole,
dirt rich with the nutrients of glaciated continents.
While digging, I prepared myself
to tackle this coming tricky part.

What's left is curled and calcified,
stored somewhere in the back of my mind.
I'll really need to push. Clench.

Breathe. I feel something dislodge. Clench.
Breathe. Like a shit brewing. Clench.
An olive-speckled egg burst from my anus
and out the leg of my shorts with a thud.

Gross.
I pick it up off the grass and crack it
above the hole as if onto a skillet.
Yolky clay drips out and splashes
at the bottom. His skull, jagged humerus,
six remaining ribs, L1 & L2, bald knee joint,
and nine toes bob to the surface,
which makes me gag and want to quickly fill the grave.
Lightning.

Another spring storm flashes by
and the ground swells with fresh water.
I pause a moment—something so simple, and yet—
but then I lose the thought, and turn in for the night.

When I wake in the morning I usually look first
into the fields, but today there's a little tuft of white hair
out in my yard where I was digging yesterday,
so I run out to it and fall to my knees to investigate.
The torn-up dirt shifts and shudders while the hair grows
and grows. It keeps growing until there's suddenly also a little glimpse
of forehead. Up it comes further, furrowed as if concentrating.

Only a few minutes pass before this weird head sprouts up
another few inches and I can see eyes, caked in dirt,
blinking furiously, and their narrowed whites
shining as if in a rage, a furious uproar—

Then his damned mouth, barking, *The gates of hell
are made of the same metal as heaven's.
Both are near. Repent, repent, bonehead—*
What the hell does that even mean?
Who does this guy think he is?
Yet I can't look away.

From up close, I watch his shoulders
shrugging off the soil with ease,
his arms pushing against the ground
as if lifting himself to his feet.

But where his hips should begin is wood,
and the skin is calloused into bark,
legs inosculated into a single trunk.

He throws up his hands and shouts,
*I have BEEN planted. So then neither
is he that planteth anything, neither
he that watereth; but God that giveth the increase,*
which I can't help but roll my eyes to and scoff at.
This obviously irritates him and he locks eyes with me
and rattles off, what I'm assuming are curses
in some unrecognizable tongue.

God, I had hoped for peace, plumcots,
potatoes at least, or anything but this frankensteining
of fronds and scripture. I back slowly into the house,
upstairs, and into bed. *Maybe this is some nightmare
I must wake from with sleep*, I wish out loud.

The next morning, garbage day, all is quiet.
Without looking out the windows, for fear of somehow confirming
yesterday, or maybe with some degree of hopeful ignorance
that the problem would have taken care of itself,
I walk outside to collect the cans and I'm greeted with pelting rocks,
stinging my face and chest, and that stupid voice again,
laughing. *You know,* I shouted, wincing, shielding
my eyes, *When I'm dead I intend to stay it,
to let life get on with itself.*

He freezes in mid throw, as if considering,
drops the rock in his hand
and proceeds to tear up the grass
within his radius in a fit of rage, muttering,
*Do not I hate them, O Lord, that hate thee?
And am not I grieved with those that rise up against thee?
I hate them with perfect hatred! I count them mine enemies!*

Through the night, he mutters and tears
the ground bare, ripping apart every blade of grass,

every root, every unfortunate weed.
When there's nothing left but dirt,
he starts shoveling that aside too,
exposing his deep seeded trunk more and more.
This goes on for days.

Then one day, I'm not sure how much later,
a pileated wood pecker swoops down and
lands on his chest as I'm watching him from inside.
He pauses and then smashes it like a mosquito.
Something in me snaps. *No!* I shout,
No! No! No! That's the last straw!

I storm from the house out to the shed
as he mockingly calls after me, *The foxes have holes,
and the birds of the air have nests;
but the Son of man hath not where to lay his head.*
I emerge with my ax and call to him, *Enough is enough!
You can lay your head in the dirt for all I care!*
I raise my ax and run at him.

I land a blow in his woody torso,
he yelps, punches me in the face once,
twice, three times before I can duck
and yank the ax away. I wind up
to swing again, but this time he catches it
by the handle and tries to yank it from my grip.
I pull back. He pulls me in so close
I can smell the petrichor on his breath.

I spit in his eyes, and he swats at me,
but I parry left, right, draw back,
and swing again.

Our shadows grow long as we fight,
which is to say that it is late, getting later,
and darkness is creeping over us,
but his eyes are murderous,
and I am enraged, and so we fight

through the night, swinging wildly
at each other with, eventually, only the moon shining
over us through cirrostratus clouds
that are growing thicker into tin-sheets of rain,
which is to say this whole ordeal sucks.

As we hack away at each other, my thoughts wander
to my siblings, to my sickly father, to my unhappy mother.
I think of European colonialism,
my childhood teachers, the meditations of lightning,
the delinquencies of dust devils, the deafening
tintinnabulations of spores whistling down to Earth
from atomic mushroom clouds, a red-rock reflection
of sky in the glass eyes of taxidermized peacocks
with a terra-cotta sunset set upon the entire flock, negative
capability, an unspanked moon harvesting
above a children's prison, the indolent bodies
of geese strung to a mobile, turning north, south,
north again, all the while I'm longing for Whitman's
beautiful uncut hair of graves,
as we fight faster and with greater hatred.

The night is growing green with dawn, the ground dews,
a chill fogs between us. Viscous, sappy blood
crystalizes all down my arms and hands.
My legs tremble with exhaustion,
but still I charge him.

Morning comes fully now,
he's teetering on a single stilt,
the sun rises like a guillotine.
To make a long story short,
I fell him.
He splinters.

For a moment, all is quiet.
   The ringing in my ears
        fades.
                I can hear bird songs again.

I am weeping.

I weep for his death.
      I weep for his resurrection.
    I weep at my strength, and I weep for my chipped blade,
  and again for his death.

Once the tears clear, I see the highway
and I can't help but imagine those passing by.

      How many others out there,
          driving along this highway right now,
     are in the final months
      of a someone's life
          or in the years that follow?

Okay, a word of advice—

    their bodies
will
    sprout up
    all around you   like thistles.

       And like thistles,
    they will cling to your socks
     and leave little splinters in your fingers,
which will linger all day
    when you try to pull them off.

But then, when you do pick them out,
    do not drop them in the dirt
 or else they will spread.
     Their roots will tunnel down quickly,
they'll invade your gardens
          no matter what you're growing,
and they'll be a bitch to clear later.

      Instead,

place them in a feeder.
Do not burn them or waste them.
                    Everything can be useful.

          Birds will gather in flocks.
And their music will begin—
and the music will say
          more than anyone can
without ever having to say a word.

Do not resurrect your dead.
The dead are dead and should remain dead.

Starting now,
this is how I'd like to rest.

Clear

Upon viewing my father's photo of an empty sky

No orange
                flares falling
from the sun,
                no stars desperate
to reach us
                on the ground,
no mountains
                unblinkingly
waiting,
                no birds migrating
back to familiar
                ponds, no trees
huddled,
                gossiping,
no planes,
                no cars,
no roads,
                no houses,
no diamonds,
                no swing-sets,
no second—
                nor third—wives,
no offices,
                no healthcare,
no check-ups,
                no shadows,
no hospitals,
                no butterfly-needles,
no blood-bags,
                no IVs,
no MRIs,
                no cancer,
no gurneys,
                no nurses,
no doctors,

                no med students,
no catheters,
                no feeding tubes,
no radiation,
                no chemo,
no surgical teams,
                no donors,
no ventilators,
                no transplants,
no mistakes,
                no suffocation,
no brain death,
                no artificial life,
no
                nothing.

In the Lens

Upon viewing Nancy Fewke's, Site A. Spring Lake, 3.17, *at the McLean County Arts Center*

This must be what Buddha sees,
the Himalayas in a spring lake
with lotus flowers, blooming
on lily pad clouds, tethered down
by chlorophyll tentacles. True,

nothing exists alone. In this picture's
reflection, the gallery,
every other piece on display—
the infinitely shining jewels
sewn into Indra's net, reflecting
me, reflecting you.

Yes, the only way to speak
of permanence
is with impermanence—
Appetite. Myth. Even mountains
erode, lilies catch disease,
lakes drain like water in cupped hands.

But for now, the flags
of triumphant climbers peak
above the atmosphere,
a peace lily spoons forward a truce
in the lobby, and right here,
sensitive, flickering, severe,
I recognize my father,
too, had an art.

In this moment, I see.

At My Father's Wake (Fields in which Laborers Detassele Corn at Random)

Your mom didn't come?
What about your brother's?
Well, I guess I can't blame them.
So it goes.
Sorry for your loss.

Memorial Day

Every year my mother would drag us to Jewel-Osco to buy wreaths of gardenias, lilies, and daises to liven up our limestone namesakes etched in those familiar cemeteries. The first, on the west side of town, across the street from Miller Park Zoo, was a type of zoo itself where all the exhibits we cared to read about were caged within marble-plated concrete slabs. The mausoleum curator would greet us at the door. Our footsteps echoed through the cold hallways as he led us straight to the Tates past rows of other entombed bodies, leaking like rusted cars in a junkyard, pooling their various fluids on the concrete below. Next, we'd visit the Dooleys' graves out in Le Roy. As we drove east on Highway 150, my mother would re-tell her story about Grandma Dooley, how, in her house dress, she once drove her long-nosed Cadillac, which was not an ordinary scene, down to Dooley Park to scold the kids bullying my mother and her brother. She would quiz me on which land our family had farmed, but the country has never stilled enough for me to remember the boundary markers. Though I do remember how I preferred the graveyard to the mausoleum, the shadows of the headstones, lengthening, smearing into the trees' across the damp quilt, tucking in and sponging dry the dead. But the day was long, and I'd often complain, wished to return home to my video games. She would tell me our dead held God's good listening ear, and that by showing up they would sing of our accomplishments. For many years, I believed her. I don't know what my father believed, but he, too, would visit those inherited plots, hear again the same stories and decided to give his body to nothing but fire—after suffering, in life, enough decay. Although I no longer visit my mother's dead, I understand now that longing to return somewhere to decorate stone with flowers.

> from my fingertips,
> his ashes grip
> the wind

Nullipara

> *At the / end of his life his life began / to wake in me.*
> —Sharon Olds

I carry my father now
inside my lungs
where he dreams
and kicks and scratches
with new fingernails.
With every labored breath
from that womb
a heat slicks my sinuses
and tongue with steam.
I choke on his name,
but exhale nothing.
When will I finally breathe
for myself, again?
BOYISH BODIES ARE NOT BUILT FOR LIFE!
Our flesh never stitches together
more, hungrier flesh.
No dormant milk ripens
around our bulk of bones.
How will I ever deliver
or abort?

Aubade

For Izzy

It's before the rusting hour I leave you
to resume my exhuming.

                    He's still strewn
beneath the surface. I have autopsied
all I've recovered thus far: eyes, hands, fume,
but it isn't enough. I need to dig
more so I can test my hypotheses,
hold his mummified skin up to lightning,
watch it crawl again.

                I've even set out
candles, written the ordered steps, sigils,
and his name in goat's blood, chanted Latin,
yet conjured nothing useful this morning.
Damn it. I think I'm the one who's possessed—

I need to write this but don't want you to
remember me how I remember him.
So, sleep for now, and leave me to my work.
When you rise, so shall I out of this dirt.

Alphabet Cone

Once I witnessed,
in a quick-receding
wash of glistening
sand and white-
marbled foam,
a small shell,
which I recognized
not only from
my field guides
but also by
my inherited love
of mollusks:
an alphabet cone,
small but weighty,
pearly-brassy,
polished in my palm,
adorned with blue-veined
beads of salt, glinting
in the midday sun.

Its cryptic pattern
of letterings—
some legible,
most not—
shone orange.
I yelled to
my father who
was bent over,
scanning the surf
ahead. He turned, picked
up his jingling bag,
and ran to me.
I offered my find
and he leaned in
to inspect it.
We both held our breath.

I cannot remember
what he said next.
This happened in Sanibel
more than a decade
ago, increasingly more
than half my life ago—
before the tense
divorce and relocation,
the confusing angst
of maturity, the cancer's
dormant birth
into his liver—
yet, this gift
from the sea
still holds
its inscription,
outlasting his life
and fiery rebirth
into sand.

It has shaped me,
although the meaning
hides itself still.
I now live
simply in the joy
of these treasures—
memories washing
ashore—welcoming
this clear tide's
decision to expose,
bury, or carry me
across the blue
horizon like a shell
painted with
the pleasures of peace
and what was,
tumbling through
the ebb and flow,
marking, forgetting,
searching, searching—

Acknowledgments

Many warms thanks to the editors of the journals who gave the following poems their first home, sometimes in different forms:

Better Than Starbucks: "October…" & "darkness…" & "flowers bloom…"
december magazine: "Shell Collecting" & " The Final Day"
Dream Pop Journal: "MRI"
Hotel Amerika: "Ventilator"
Midwest Writing Center: "His Iowa Friends"
Modern Haiku: "like gardeners…" & "sunrise…" & "they march single-file…" & "a ball of twine…"
Plainsong: "Sometime After My Father Died"
Sulphur Surrealist Jungle: "Nullipara" & "What's Left" & "Peonies in Reverse"
SurVision Magazine: "To My Father's Roses"
Texas Poetry Calendar: "sudden rain…" & "windy morning…"
The American Journal of Poetry & Dispatches from the Poetry Wars: "I Dreamt Us Having a Pure Son and Father Moment"
The Ekphrastic Review: "Pure Land"
The Loch Raven Review: "My Father's Needlepointed Santa Lumbar Pillow"
The Thieving Magpie: "Crows" & "Blackbird"

There are many people who I'm fortunate to call my friends, who've dedicated their time to these poems over the years. All of whom are responsible, in one way or another, for this final product, and for molding me into the writer I am today. Thank you, William Brown, Bob Carroll, Joanne Diaz, Tao Jin, Jake Lewis, Claire Martin, Sarah Pila, Brandi Reissenweber, Alison Sainsbury, Austin Smith, Mike Theune, and Rachel Jamison Webster. I am immensely grateful to each and every one you for your attentive eyes and compelling encouragements.

Thank you to the editors at Finishing Line Press for finding something in my work worth pursuing, particularly to Christen Kincaid for her detailed and dedicated attention to these poems as they shifted and grew in many different directions during the editorial process.

My gratitude goes out to the many poets whose work sustained me through this process, but especially to Cornelius Eady, Kent Johnson, and Sharon Olds. Thank you for writing with such identifiable familiarity to a grief I've also come to call my own.

But, most of all, my appreciation belongs to my fierce-loving, strong-hearted wife, Izzy. Your encouragement during my father's sickness and every day after, your lifting and pushing me forward, your constant presence made all of this possible, and makes it worth something. I know Dad would love you now if he had the chance to get to know you then.

And now, reader, my father belongs to you.

Tate Lewis-Carroll (they/them), husband, chicken farmer, Starbucks barista, an internationally published poet with works translated into Arabic, serves as Poetry Editor for the *Ocotillo Review* and as an Editor for Kallisto Gaia Press. They've received an Honorable Mention for the 2022 James Tate International Chapbook Prize. They are the editor of the *2022 Texas Poetry Calendar* anthology. Their work has been anthologized in *Contemporary Surrealist and Magic Realist Poets* (Lamar University Press) and also appears in *Hotel Amerika, Frogpond, Modern Haiku, december magazine,* and others. They live on a small farm in central Illinois with their photographer wife, Izzy, and miles in-between the nearest towns. Find them on Instagram: @TateLewisCarroll, Twitter: TPLPoetry, or somewhere out in the woods.

www.ingramcontent.com/pod-product-compliance
Lightning Source LLC
Chambersburg PA
CBHW042139160426
43200CB00020B/2982